Power

D1644526

Machiavelli

Power

GET IT, USE IT, KEEP IT

➼><◅

P
PROFILE BOOKS

First published in Great Britain in 2001 by
Profile Books Ltd
58A Hatton Garden
London ECIN 8LX
www.profilebooks.co.uk

Introduction and text selection copyright
© Jeremy Scott 2001

Text extracts selected from the *The Prince* by
Niccolò Machiavelli; folio translation of 1674,
reprinted by Routledge in 1883.

A CIP catalogue record for this book is available from the
British Library.

ISBN 1 86197 353 5

Cover design by the Senate
Cover and frontispiece illustration by Clifford Harper
Text design by Geoff Green
Typeset in Van Dijck by MacGuru
info@macguru.org.uk

Printed and bound in Great Britain by
Bookmarque Ltd, Croydon, Surrey

Contents

Of middle height, slender figure, lively eyes, black hair, small head, a slightly aquiline nose, a firmly closed mouth; all about him gave the impression of a very acute observer and thinker. But he could not always suppress the sarcastic expression playing around his mouth and visible in his eyes . . .

Niccolò Machiavelli was born in 1469, at the height of the Renaissance – a period of such vitality, progress and rapid change that it did not merely transform Italy, but awoke the whole western world to new life. For a talented or clever man, this was a time of unlimited opportunity.

The republic of Florence, controlled by Lorenzo de Medici, was immensely rich from industry and trade, but above all from finance. Commerce boomed, art and learning prospered, pornography flourished; all shared a permissive extravagance and zest to live.

But not Machiavelli, who was excluded from this rich feast. Born into a family which had known grander and better times, his childhood was passed not in absolute poverty, but in severely restricted circumstances. His father, a lawyer, had been barred from public office as an insolvent debtor.

On the small farm near Florence where Machiavelli was raised, life was frugal and lived close to the bone. He 'learnt to do without before he learnt to enjoy'. Little money was available; he could not afford the classes attended by his fashionable peer group, the children of the city's leading families. Unlike theirs, his teachers were undistinguished. But his home, though poor in every other respect, was rich in books. And these – especially history – he read voraciously. Driven by ambition, Machiavelli educated himself; he was a self-made man.

In *The Prince*, the book in which Machiavelli set down his principles for achieving power and success, he says that to have ability alone is not enough, but that Fortuna – opportunity – is also needed. Fortuna smiled on Machiavelli at 29 when he was given an important job in the Florentine civil service.

He was working for a new administrator; the Medicis had now fallen from power and been exiled. Ruling the republic was a high-risk game. A wood merchant, interrogated about the death of the Duke of Gandia, said he had 'seen in his day a hundred corpses thrown into the river at that spot, and no questions asked about them'.

Machiavelli proved himself a conscientious and effective bureaucrat in this menacing political climate. His job was soon extended to include foreign affairs.

Florence's relationships with the powers around her were unstable and fraught with danger. The Italian peninsula was divided into independent states; among them, Florence was hugely prosperous. Her strength lay in her wealth, her weakness in the fact that she had no army of her own and depended upon mercenary troops.

Yet Florence was surrounded by neighbours who were not friendly. The chief problem was how to keep open her only access to the sea, which ran through Pisa, a subsidiary state demanding self-government and becoming increasingly difficult to control.

Machiavelli's first diplomatic mission was to Forlì and its ruler, the redoubtable Caterina

Sforza. Machiavelli's instructions were to try to obtain mercenary troops, buy as much gunpowder as Caterina would sell, and prevent her from signing an alliance with Milan.

Caterina's reputation for determination was enough to make any novice diplomat nervous. While pregnant by the first of three husbands and away from Forlì, she had heard that her castle had been seized by its custodian. She had flung herself into the saddle to ride there, arrested him, tied him to a horse and hauled the traitor back for punishment. Next day, she gave birth.

Negotiating with the still inexperienced Machiavelli, Caterina claimed to have no gunpowder to spare but agreed to supply troops. Machiavelli at once sent a letter to Florence reporting his success, but next day she announced to his dismay that she had changed her mind. He was young enough to remind her of her promise of the night before, and was told, 'Secretary, you are wrong to be surprised at the alteration; the more such things are considered, the better are they understood.'

Finally Caterina decided that she might

come to terms if Florence would guarantee to protect her territory. But this was outside Machiavelli's brief and his mission was an apparent failure. Yet Caterina had been impressed by him and remained on friendly terms with Florence.

Machiavelli's next mission was to Louis XII, King of France. Machiavelli was the junior of two envoys; the legation was led by the better-born Della Casa. Their instructions were to settle a dispute over who was to pay for the mercenary forces which Louis had supplied in the unsuccessful siege of Pisa.

The French court's attitude towards the two Florentines was supercilious and contemptuous. In a letter home, Machiavelli says they were treated like country bumpkins.

Della Casa fell ill and returned to Italy. Pursuing the mission alone, Machiavelli was miserably short of funds. Nothing, he reported, could be achieved without bribery, which he was not equipped to offer, but in time his perseverance paid off. The French king's financial demands were settled, and in return Machiavelli achieved a diplomatic coup. France would guarantee Florence's borders against the mounting threat from Cesare Borgia. A friend wrote to congratulate Machiavelli on his success. A postscript in a woman's hand adds that he's sadly missed in Florence where 'a certain person awaits him with wide-open legs . . .'

The danger posed by Borgia had been long foreseen by Machiavelli. Borgia and his sister Lucrezia were the children of the reigning pope, a man unusually corrupt and depraved even for those excessive times. It was said that both he and Borgia had incestuous relations with Lucrezia, who took many lovers, poisoned several and was violently widowed twice before her third marriage at the age of 23. Very beautiful and a born intriguer, she played a willing role as partner in their schemes.

Borgia, charismatic, handsome and cunning, took the lead. The pope had created him a cardinal aged seventeen and at 24 he'd switched careers to become captain-general of the papal army in Romagna, adjacent to Florence. Very quickly his pitiless methods subdued disorder, imposing peace and with it prosperity. He then took over three further city states, whose inhabitants welcomed him as their liberator.

Borgia was an able administrator, though utterly ruthless. While absent from Romagna, he learned that the governor he'd installed there was creating a problem with the inhabitants. At dawn the man's body was found in the main square hacked into two pieces.

On a mission to Borgia, Machiavelli was with him when the ruler learned of an assassination plot, and saw how he dealt with the matter. He describes how Borgia invited the plotters to dinner, received them courteously – and had them strangled.

Machiavelli relates the story in awe, even respect. He increasingly admired Borgia. It was a sort of hero-worship, the admiration of the intellectual for the charismatic man of action. When, years later, Machiavelli wrote his celebrated book, it was Borgia who was his model for the Prince.

Then the pope and Borgia were poisoned at another meal. Ironically, although many wished them gone, the poisoning was accidental. The pope died and Borgia was mortally ill for weeks, while all Italy plotted against him.

The new pope was a declared enemy of Borgia. Machiavelli, now attached to the papal court at Rome, watched the progressive ruination of his hero until, humiliated and stripped of all power, Borgia ended up in prison.

Machiavelli's own career, though, continued to flourish. Its high point was setting up a national militia that was used to assault Pisa, which Florence had been trying to recover for fifteen years. The new force was successful and there were immense celebrations in Florence; bonfires blazed in the streets and Machiavelli was hailed as the 'organiser of victory'. It was the most triumphant moment of his life.

Then, abruptly, the power balance changed again. Lorenzo de Medici returned as head of a new government. Machiavelli was fired from all his posts. Then a plot against Lorenzo was discovered and a list of names seized, Machiavelli's among them. He was arrested and tortured, enduring four 'twists of the rack' before he was eventually released.

Ruined and disgraced, Machiavelli retired to the small family farm near Florence where he was born. He was 44; he had a wife and five children. Now in desperate straits, he was summoned for non-payment of taxes. A friend, writing to certify Machiavelli's inability to pay, testified, 'He's really poor, as I can affirm, penniless and burdened with children.' Thanking this friend, Machiavelli says, 'I would be better dead, and my family better without me, since I am only a burden, being accustomed to spend and unable to exist without spending.'

Machiavelli's poverty and exile in his little farmhouse at San Casciano continued until he died there at the age of 58. Yet during his exile he found salvation in writing, and also won himself a name in history. He wrote about what he knew: power, the science to which he'd devoted his life and at which – although he'd never wanted it for himself – he was so brilliantly adept. The archetypal backroom strategist, Machiavelli was, and is, the acknowledged master of the subject.

In exile, Machiavelli explains
his life . . . and dedicates
his handbook

-->-<-

I rise with the sun and go into my woods which I am having cut down; I examine the work done the day before and exchange idle gossip with the woodcutters, who are always engaged in some new dispute either between themselves or with their neighbours.

Leaving the wood, I carry a book with me to a shady spot by a spring where I read, usually Dante or Petrarch or one of the minor classical poets. Seated on the bank I follow their passions and their love affairs, recall my own, and take pleasure for a while in the thought of them.

Then I move on to the inn where I chat with those stopping there, hear news of the places they have travelled through, and observe the different tastes and humours of mankind.

It is time to dine. I go home and sit down with my family to eat the simple food my meagre circumstances can afford.

After dinner I return to the inn. There,

generally, I find the host, a butcher, a miller and one or two charcoal-burners. With them I play at dice amid swearing, insults and arguments over a penny so loud our shouting can be heard as far as San Casciano. In this trivial way I try to keep my brain from going mouldy. But Fortune is perverse in the way she acts! I submit to her driving me along this wretched path to see if she will not become ashamed of what she's doing.

When evening comes I return home and remove my muddy clothes to put on clean attire. Thus well-dressed, in the privacy of my study I enter the courts of men in history. Welcomed by them, I converse, listen to their talk, and do not hesitate to question them on the reasons why in their time they acted in such or such a way. In their amiability they reply to me. For the space of four hours I feel no fatigue, I forget all my troubles, I do not fear poverty, and death no longer affrights me. I am exalted and inspired.

I have listened to these men attentively, noting down all the more significant points of their conversation, and have assembled a little book which I call 'The Prince'. In this I have delved as deeply as I can into the subject of power. I examine the nature of a principality, the different types of principality, how power is to be won, how retained, and how it may be lost.

I hope this little book will please you, and prove useful to a new Prince . . .

Machiavelli's basic terms

>><<

*T*he woman or man to whom his book is addressed, that is to say the individual who already holds power or wishes to seize it, Machiavelli calls the PRINCE.

The corporation or other organisation which the Prince controls or wants to control, he terms the STATE.

*T*he Prince's necessary characteristics

→>·<←

Virtù: Not 'virtue' as we understand the word today, but courage, ability, cunning and ruthless determination — plus a certain flame within.

Fortuna: Luck and opportunity.

I think it is probably true to say that Fortuna governs one half of our actions, but that we ourselves have control of the other half.

It is better to be bold than timid, for Fortuna is a woman. And, like a woman, she prefers young men, because they are less cautious, more ardent, and more daring in their demands.

The end justifies the means

➤>-◄-

Of course we're all aware how admirable and praiseworthy it is considered for a Prince to live her or his life in an ethical, honest, and open manner.

Nevertheless, we can't help observing that nowadays those Princes who care little about principle and integrity but instead make use of cunning and deceit obtain wealth, celebrity and great success. They achieve very much more than those who base their conduct upon openness and honesty . . .

Strategy of power

→>-<←

There are two ways to conduct a conflict: by lawful means, or by the use of force.

The first is considered appropriate to women and men, and the second to beasts. But often the first method is ineffective, and it becomes necessary to adopt the second.

And so it is necessary that a Prince must know how to employ both the man and the beast within. She or he must learn to make proper use of both these natures, for one will not remain effective for long without the help of the other.

Be both fox and lion

As it is essential for a Prince to learn the use of the beast, she or he should imitate both the fox and the lion as models. For the lion is in danger from traps, and the fox cannot defend himself from wolves. So a Prince should be fox enough to spot and evade the traps, and lion enough to scare off wolves.

To model yourself on the lion alone is not enough.

Duplicity

A wise Prince cannot and should not keep her or his word when it is disadvantageous to do so, and when the circumstances and reasons for that original promise no longer apply.

If people were honest and straightforward this would be the wrong advice to give. But we all know this is not the case; they are unscrupulous and bad. They would break their promises to you, so you are under no obligation to keep faith with them.

Seem to be good . . .

A Prince need not really possess all the good qualities but she or he must *seem* to possess them. I will even go further and say that if he has them and insists always on practising them they will harm his position, whereas if he merely seems to have them he will profit from them.

Ideally the Prince should really have those virtues, but know how to adopt contrary qualities when the situation requires. For a Prince, and especially a new Prince, will often be obliged in order to retain power to violate good faith, truth, kindness and humanity. And so he must be prepared to adapt his behaviour as circumstances change. He should be good when he can but wicked as is necessary.

. . . never show you are not

A Prince must take care always to appear and sound like a person of integrity, honesty, kindness and humanity.

People judge only by their eyes, for all can see the appearance, but few know the reality. Everyone sees what you seem to be, few discern what you really are; and those few will not dare to contradict the masses, who have the majesty of the Prince on their side.

The actions of all people, but especially of Princes, are judged only by their results.

So a Prince must do whatsoever is expedient and necessary to gain and keep power; the means she or he uses will always be considered honourable – provided they are successful.

Consolidating power by the use of cruelty

→>—<←

Private persons who become Princes through the favour of Fortuna meet with few obstacles in their rise to power, but with many problems in maintaining their position and holding on to that power after they have achieved it.

It is easy on the way up but their power can have no firm base unless they at once set about constructing solid foundations to their position.

After the coup

With states that are newly conquered which have been accustomed to liberty and lived under their own laws, there is a choice of three ways to follow.

The first is utterly to ruin them. The second to live personally among them and rule. The third is for the Prince to allow them to continue under their own laws, setting up a government to keep them obedient and loyal.

Eliminating dissent

From the study of Roman history we know that when the form of government changes in a state (whether from a republic to a tyranny or *vice versa*), it is essential to take exemplary action against those hostile to the new rule.

The Prince who institutes a new government without killing Brutus and the sons of Brutus will not remain in power for long.

Cruelty

It may seem strange that wicked, treacherous Princes who practise atrocities not only prosper at home but also triumph against foreign enemies. Many cruel rulers manage to retain power throughout times of peace, as well as in war.

But this depends on whether they use cruelty correctly, or incorrectly . . .

Correct and incorrect use

Cruelties used correctly are those done for the reason of self-survival. They are exacted on a single occasion, decisively, once and for all.

Cruelty wrongly used is that which is slight at first, but which increases over the course of time, rather than diminishing.

Princes who employ the first method often are successful; those who follow the second must always keep their knife in hand.

Cruelty must be swift . . .

When a Prince seizes power in a state, she or he should decide what cruelties are necessary – then carry them out decisively in a single day. Afterwards they will have time and opportunity to secure the loyalty of their subjects through generosity, appointments, and favours.

A Prince too timid to act in this decisive fashion must always watch his back and can never wholly trust or rely upon her or his subjects.

. . . reward can be slow

Executions and punishments should be sudden and performed all at once. Rewards on the other hand should be drop by drop, so their benefits may be spread out over a long while.

Playing off management
against the workforce

+>-<+

It sometimes happens that an individual becomes Prince of a state not through wickedness or force but by the choice of its inhabitants.

In this case it will require not just Fortuna and Virtù but a particular sort of cunning to govern such a state, for the Prince has been raised to power by the support of only one of the two different groups that form it.

That is to say the Prince is backed either by the populace, or by the nobles . . .

Hostility between the two

In such a state conflict inevitably exists between these two groups, because the populace do not want to be oppressed by the nobles, while the nobles want to dominate and exploit the populace.

A Prince who achieves power through the backing of the nobles will experience greater difficulties than if promoted by the people; for the new Prince will be surrounded by many old associates who believe they are as capable as she or he is and are not prepared to be told what to do.

Danger in each

In the other case, where a Prince is raised to power by the people, he stands above them and alone. All, or almost all, are ready to obey him.

The worst a Prince has to fear from the people is that they may desert him; whereas the nobles may collude and rebel against him.

The people he cannot alter, he must accept them as they are. But with the nobles it is different; he can manipulate them by the gift of power, honour, favours . . . or dismiss them as he pleases.

Senior executives

The nobles are made up of two groups: those who commit fully to you, and those who do not.

Those who commit (so long as they are capable and not dishonest) should be loved and honoured by the Prince.

Those who withhold commitment can be divided into two sorts . . .

Caution . . . or ambition?

Some nobles withhold commitment through caution, or laziness. These the Prince should make use of, provided they are capable, for she or he has nothing to fear from them.

But if the reason a noble avoids committing to the Prince is due to his own ambition, then the Prince must guard against him as an outright enemy. For, given the opportunity, that noble will conspire to ruin him.

*W*inning popularity

❧❧❧

If an individual becomes Prince of a state through the support of the nobles, but against the wishes of the people, his first goal must be to become loved by them.

This love and popularity can be easily obtained by giving them security and welfare. If these are bestowed at a moment when they were expecting not generosity but cruelty and oppression, they will come to love and honour that Prince even more than if they had elected him themselves.

Charisma, public relations
and management style

→>-<←

A Prince who is the existing ruler of a state already possesses and is demonstrating to all a characteristic personal style.

But a new Prince must deliberately set out to create her or his distinctive personal charisma . . .

Inventing enemies

When Fortuna wishes to smile upon a Prince she manufactures enemies so the Prince may gain in glory by overcoming them.

So a shrewd Prince should at times encourage some disaffection so she or he can demonstrate how effective they are in resolving the problem.

Reward, recognition and office parties

A Prince should recognise achievement in his subjects and reward excellence. At appropriate moments she or he should also provide feasts and celebrations for the people.

And, since all states are divided into different departments, he should pay due attention to each, and attend their gatherings occasionally to display his benevolence and affability, always however maintaining the dignity of his position, which must never be compromised in any way whatever.

After the coup

If an individual becomes the Prince of a state which she or he intends to run dishonestly and for their own profit, the best course to follow is to change everything from top to bottom, instituting new officials, new titles and new systems.

Nothing should be left as it was before; the Prince must ensure that everyone who holds power or wealth owes it directly to him and no one else.

New disciplines

It is damaging for a Prince to bring in a new law which is generally disregarded and not observed by her or his people.

And if the Prince does not personally observe this law it will bring reproach and do her or him great harm by ruining their reputation.

Danger in absolute power

If a Prince takes over a state whose people were accustomed to a degree of liberty, then tries to impose a system of absolute rule, she or he risks to run into difficulties. For if the state is administered by senior officials the Prince will be obliged to rely upon their continuing loyalty and goodwill; and in times of trouble they can ruin him, by either ignoring or defying his orders.

State of emergency

If the state is governed by senior officials the people may not be prepared to obey the Prince's authority if a state of emergency arises. In the event he cannot rely upon the people; in peace and prosperity all promise to die for him, but in a crisis few will be ready to do so.

For a Prince to bypass his senior officials and make a direct appeal to the population is very dangerous, for it can only be made once.

New systems

A Prince is at risk when she or he attempts to introduce new systems. Those who profited from the old will hate him, while those who will run the new are uncommitted and lukewarm.

The Prince will receive little support until such systems are seen to function successfully.

Fate of the Prince's ally

Whoever is the cause of a Prince coming into power is as a result usually ruined themselves. For they have assisted the Prince through the use of either strength or guile, and both of these become suspect to the Prince after she or he is established in power.

Loyalty

＊＞＜＊

To be truly secure in her or his rule a wise Prince must make certain that his citizens are constantly in need of his protection and benefit. If this is so, then they will always remain loyal to him.

Choosing executives

✦✦✦✦

A Prince's selection of her or his ministers is of paramount importance.

People will judge a Prince on whether or not he has shown wisdom in choosing them.

Character in ministers

A Prince need not possess high intellect himself, but must have the shrewdness to recognise ability in others. She or he must be able to identify their strengths and weaknesses, and use them accordingly. Thus the minister, knowing that he is known, will not try to deceive the Prince but serve her or him well despite their natural inclination.

Types of applicant

Those who seek office from the Prince are of three sorts.

One has the intelligence to understand a matter her or himself; others can understand when it has been explained to them; others are capable of neither.

The first is excellent, the second useful, the rest fools.

Trust

If a minister is ambitious to advance her or himself and seeks his own advantage in a matter entrusted to him, he will never be reliable and the Prince can never trust him.

A good minister thinks only and always of his Prince, and never troubles him with anything inessential.

Loyalty

A wise Prince will love and reward a loyal minister, heaping riches, honours, and title upon them. Thus the minister will depend wholly upon the Prince, because he stands to forfeit all by political change.

In such a relationship the Prince and minister may safely trust each other.

Advisors and advice

━►━◄━

If a Prince without great wisdom of his own relies on many ministers to advise him their advice will inevitably differ and conflict, for each is thinking of her or his own agenda.

As a result the Prince will not understand the true nature of any situation, and will not be able to act appropriately.

A premier minister?

A Prince who is not wise himself can never receive good counsel unless he has the benefit of an individual minister of great ability who advises him on everything.

In such case he will be well guided, but not for long, for that minister will become Prince in her or his place.

Flattery

Flattery is a great danger for a Prince, for every court is filled with flatterers. She or he can make it known that everyone should tell them the truth, but if all feel free to do so they will lose respect for him.

A Prince should therefore follow another way, by choosing wise ministers who are free to tell him the truth – but only about those matters on which he consults them and no others.

Decisiveness

A Prince should encourage her or his ministers to speak freely on an issue; then, when he has heard them out, announce his decision firmly and permit no further debate.

Otherwise, he will be either brought to ruin by those who tell him what they think he wishes to hear, or held in contempt because of his indecisiveness.

Wisdom

To conclude the subject of advisors, I would say that good counsel from whatever source has its origin in the natural wisdom of the Prince, rather than the wisdom of the Prince resulting from good advice from others.

Relationship with employees

+>-<+

A Prince should take the greatest care to avoid doing anything which risks to excite his people's hatred or contempt.

Above all she or he must not cheat their subjects; for the majority of people will live and work contentedly so long as their wealth and self-respect remain undamaged.

If the majority are content then the risk of dissension lies only in the ambitions of a small minority, and this can be easily controlled in several ways . . .

Particular circumstances

A Prince should be aware that hatred may be excited by his following the honourable course as well as through choosing the wicked one.

To hold on to power the Prince will at times be obliged to embrace evil. For, if the faction who support the Prince is corrupt, she or he must collude with this corruption to keep them loyal.

To act honourably in such a case will only harm him.

Healthy fear

It is entirely possible for a Prince to be feared without being hated, provided he does not steal the property and women of his subjects; and if he has to put anyone to death, he does so only where there is clear reason to do so.

Nobility

A Prince will come into contempt if he is seen to be indecisive or changeable or timorous.

She or he must ensure that all their actions reflect greatness, courage, and strength. A Prince must never alter his decisions, and his reputation must be such that no one would think of deceiving him.

A ruler who achieves this will be highly respected. It is very hard to mount a conspiracy against him or to attack him.

Consistency

Finally in this matter of a Prince's relationship with her or his subjects, I would add that it is essential to be always consistent.

In good times and in bad he must be the same toward them. In the bad times it serves for nothing to punish his subjects; and now to reward them with promotions and honours will cause them to feel no gratitude but only to despise him, for they see him to be fearful and needy.

Conspiracy

✦>✦<✦

Two things a Prince has to fear are rebellion within her or his state, and an attack from outside.

If the foundation to his power is sound all will be well internally so long as he is not undermined by conspiracy; and even if attacked from outside his borders he will be able to overcome, so long as he observes the principles I have prescribed.

But even if there is no external threat, some of his subjects may still mount a conspiracy against him. He can guard against this in several ways . . .

Be loved —
choose others to be hated

A Prince has no cause to fear conspiracies if she or he enjoys the love and respect of his people; but if they hate or despise him he has much to fear from everyone.

For this reason he should entrust unpopular measures to others, and reserve popular ones for himself.

Prime protection

The best protection a Prince can erect for her or himself is to be loved and admired by their subjects. For if conspirators see the fall of the Prince will be unpopular with the masses this will discourage them from mounting a coup against him.

Nature of conspiracy

Conspiracies are always hazardous for those who engage in them. Many are recorded by history, but few have been successful. A conspirator requires supporters, and in recruiting them he lays himself open to betrayal and very great dangers.

Conspirators live in continual fear of exposure and punishment, which can only inhibit them; while the Prince has on his side status, the law, authority, and friends.

If she or he has in addition the love of their people, no one will be so rash as to mount a conspiracy against them.

Paranoia

A Prince should not be too ready to credit informants or to believe in plots, or allow himself to become paranoid. She or he has little to fear while the population are at ease, but when they are not he should keep his dagger to hand.

The constant care of a wise Prince in a well-governed state must be not to reduce the nobles to despair nor the people to discontent.

Attack and defence

✦

As I have explained, a principality must have strong foundations and efficient internal government or its ruin is certain.

When those foundations are in place, the government functioning effectively and the people content, a Prince should then have no other thought in her or his mind than that of war.

War is a Prince's function; it supports his position and increases his reputation. Princes who indulge themselves in pleasures instead of waging war often forfeit their states; indeed the neglect of war is the principal reason that princedoms are lost.

Therefore to complete this handbook I will discuss the question of armed forces, and the offensive and defensive measures available to the Prince . . .

Timing the assault

If the Prince desires to gain some advantage from the ruler of another state he should wherever possible give no notice of his intent but act in such a way that it requires a rapid decision from that ruler.

If the ruler sees that to refuse or delay his decision will anger the Prince, and that this may be dangerous, he will yield to what the Prince desires.

Lawyers, accountants, merchant banks

The armed forces a Prince deploys in times of war are either his own or brought in as hired mercenaries.

Mercenary forces are unreliable and dangerous. A Prince who relies on them will never be secure in power, for such forces are undisciplined, treacherous, and ambitious only for their own gain.

. . . *and again*

The commanders of mercenary forces talk and behave boldly when with their employer and their allies, but are cowards when faced by the enemy.

They have no love for the Prince, and their only reason to fight for him is what they are paid, which is never enough to make them willing to die for him.

They are glad to serve him during times of peace, but if war comes they will either desert him at once or run away in the first battle.

Ability

Something else must be said about the danger of employing mercenary forces: Their commanders are either men of ability, or they are not.

In the first case the Prince cannot trust them, for their only motive is to grow rich by exploiting her or him. In the second, they will ruin him through their habitual incompetence.

Alliances

A Prince should never make an offensive alliance with a ruler more powerful than her or himself. For if the enterprise is a success he will be subordinate to that ruler and will experience increasing problems.

Discrimination: choose to fight only battles you can win

The desire to gain territory is right and proper for a Prince, and when Princes achieve this objective successfully they are praised by everyone.

But when they are perceived by the people to be very ambitious for territory yet unable to achieve their end, they are looked on with contempt.

Furthermore, this being the Prince's own fault, she or he is to be censured for it.

A final caution

⇥⇥⇤⇤

To conclude this handbook on power I must deliver a final warning . . .

In a state where the citizens are prosperous and relatively free there is no more certain way to ruin that state than for the Prince to propose bold enterprises. For such proposals will almost always receive popular support in the emotion of the moment, and the advice of those who oppose the enterprise will be discounted.

History shows us that rash enterprises very often cause the ruin of the state, but invariably they result in the downfall and ruin of the Prince. For in these situations the people look on victory as certain – and if the Prince disappoints them they will punish that Prince with exile, imprisonment, or death.

Postscript: the lesson to be learned

━┿━

The Prince Borgia acquired his state through the influence of his father, the Pope, and lost it when that influence failed on his father's death.

This occurred despite the fact that Borgia had done all that a capable, clever woman or man can do to secure their power in a state which conflict and the help of others has given them.

We have noted in these pages that the Prince who does not lay down the foundations to her or his power beforehand can construct them afterwards only by exceptional ability. If we consider the methods employed by Borgia we can see how very solid and correct were the foundations he put down.

I know of no better example for a new Prince to follow. If his methods in the end were not successful and he ended in ruin this was through no fault of his own but only the extraordinary malignity of Fortune.

Other titles from the 'Illuminations' series

Love
by Vatsyayana
The Indian sage and compiler of the world-renowned *Kama Sutra* presents his stimulating and enduring guide to erotic technique.
ISBN 1 86197 358 6

Happiness
by Marcus Aurelius
The Roman philosopher-emperor describes his Method to achieve happiness, find inner peace and change your life for the better.
ISBN 1 86197 367 5

Faith
by St Paul
The renowned spiritual teacher explains how to find and keep to the path that leads to life after death.
ISBN 1 86197 372 1